GREENWICH LIBRARIES

PROJECT LOANS SERVICE
WEST GREENWICH LIBRARY
GREENWICH HIGH ROAD
LONDON
SE10 8NN

TEL: 081-853 1691

Please quote number and last date stamped
if you wish to renew by post or telephone

FIND OUT ABOUT

changes

Godfrey Hall

© **Godfrey Hall / BBC Education 1994**

Reprinted 1997

BBC Education
201 Wood Lane
London W12 7TS

ISBN 0 563 39615 6

Editor: Christina Digby
Designer: Claire Robertson
Picture research: Helen Taylor
Series consultant: Mary Hoffman
Educational advisers: Su Hurrell and Samina Miller
Photographers: John Jefford, Robert Pickett, Betty Press (page 7 only)
Illustrator: Philip Dobree

With grateful thanks to:
Robert Lee, Rachael Malicki

Printed in Belgium by Proost

Contents

ᨑᨑᨑᨑᨑᨑᨑᨑ

You can **change** the **shape** of a balloon in many ways. How is the shape of these balloons being changed?

What is change?

A change is when something becomes different. Chewing a piece of bread changes the way it looks and feels.

Change can happen in many ways. It can take place by heating, cooling, stretching or bending things.

Some changes produce new things. If you mix flour and water to make a dough, then heat it in an oven, you will change it into something which looks and feels different.

Sometimes you can change a thing into something else, then change it back again. You end up with what you started with. Water can be turned into ice, and ice can be turned back into water.

This lolly has been left in the **freezer** for a long time. Can you see the **ice** pattern?

The **hot** flame **melts** the candle wax.

If you take an ice cream out into the **warm** sunshine it starts to **melt** and go runny. It is changing into a **liquid**. The cornet gets warm, but does not melt.

Hard butter **melts** if you spread it on a piece of **warm** toast.

What does heat do?

Heat makes things warm. You can feel the heat from the sun on a warm day.

The heat from the sun can warm chocolate, making it soft and sometimes even runny. This is called melting.

We use heat at home to keep us warm, and to cook food.

Heat changes some things for ever. When you cook an egg by heating, it cannot be changed back to a raw egg.

On a very hot day the heat from the sun can **melt** the tar on the road. The tar goes **soft** and the top of the road can **change shape**. When the tar **cools** down, it goes **hard** again.

steam

steam

**bubbles release
water vapour**

bubbles

hot water

heat —————

What happens when water is heated?

When water is heated inside a kettle, it starts to bubble. The bubbles contain water vapour, which is very hot. Water vapour is like air, because we can't see it. When the bubbles get to the top of the water, they let the water vapour out. Now the water is boiling.

As soon as the water vapour leaves the bubble and goes into the air it starts to cool. You start to see steam as the water vapour starts to cool. We can see steam because it is made up of tiny water droplets. If steam touches something cooler, the tiny droplets join together to make bigger droplets. Have you ever seen drops of water on the window of a steamy bathroom?

Ice is **frozen** water.

When ice is **heated**, it turns back to **liquid** water.

When all the **water** has turned to **steam** the pan is dry.

Fill an ice cube tray with **water**. Ask an **adult** to place it in a freezer.

The **water** will get very cold and **freeze**. It will change to **ice cubes**.

Ask the **adult** to remove the ice cube tray from the freezer. Draw on the ice cubes with felt tip pens.

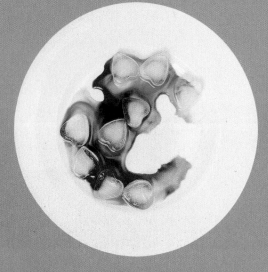

Leave the **ice cubes** in a **warm** room. How do they change?

Don't use ice cubes in your drinks after you have drawn on them.

What happens when water freezes and ice melts?

When water gets very cold, it freezes. It changes from water to ice. Water is runny and can be poured. It is a liquid. Ice is hard and cannot be poured. It is a solid.

When ice cubes are taken out of the freezer they melt and change back to water. If the same water is put back into the freezer, it changes into ice cubes again.

Fill a small plastic bottle to the top with coloured water. Do not put the lid on. Ask an adult to place the bottle upright in the freezer. Leave it overnight. Ask an adult to take the bottle out and see what has happened.

Ice takes up **more space** than **water**. The frozen water does not fit into the bottle, and comes out of the top.

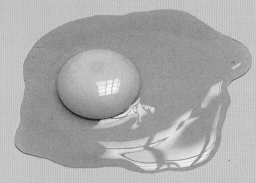

A **fried** egg cannot be changed back to a **raw** egg.

A loaf of **bread** cannot be turned back to **dough**.

How can you tell the **tomato** and the **chicken** have been **cooked**?

What does cooking do?

Cooking changes the way food looks, tastes and feels.

Cooking makes some foods soft. Raw carrots are hard. When they have been cooked, they are soft. What other foods go soft when they have been cooked?

When you cook cake mixture you have to heat it. Heat causes the runny mixture to turn into a solid cake. Heat causes the change from a liquid to a solid. The cake cannot be turned back into flour, eggs, butter and sugar.

Look at the **cake mixture** and see how it has **changed** after **cooking**.

fridge

eggs

ice box

cheese and butter

quiche

cooked meat

mi

fresh vegetables

orang juice

What happens in the fridge?

When we put food in a fridge it is kept cool. It stays fresh and lasts longer than food in a cupboard.

Food can change when it is put into a fridge. It gets cold and some food goes hard. Butter goes hard. Chocolate goes hard and brittle.

Some parts of the fridge are cooler than others. Different foods need to be kept in different parts of the fridge. Raw meat needs to be kept very cold. Fresh food that is not kept in a fridge soon goes mouldy.

Can you see the **mould** on these vegetables?

Never touch mouldy food. It can make you very ill.

A **wet** dog looks
and feels
different from a
dry dog.

The **hair** may
look **darker** and
is not fluffy.

The dog has not
soaked up the water.
Some water has
stayed on the
dog's coat, and some
has **dripped off**.

What happens when things get wet?

When things get wet they look and feel different.

Some things, like sponges, soak up water. A wet sponge is darker and heavier than a dry sponge.

Some things do not soak up water. Water stays on the outside or runs off. Some fabrics are shiny and water runs off them. These fabrics are waterproof. We use them to make raincoats.

Put different types of paper in a bowl of water. How do they change? You could try this with different types of fabric, plastic and wood. What do you notice?

The beans have been left in **water** overnight. They are **bigger** because they have **soaked up** water.

On a warm day, the **water** in the clothes is **warmed** and it turns into **tiny invisible droplets**. These are carried away in the air.

Where does water go?

When we leave things in air they can dry out. Wet clothes hung on the washing line on a warm and windy day soon dry.

Some things take longer to dry out. Flowers and fruit contain water, but they take longer to dry than clothes.

If flowers are left in the air for a long time without water, they dry and become hard. As the flowers dry, they become brittle and crisp. If touched they break easily into tiny pieces.

After a rain shower, find a **puddle**. Draw round the edge with a piece of chalk. Look at the puddle a day later. Has it changed in **size**? If it is **smaller**, where has the **water** gone?

Drop a blob of **paint** or **ink** into a glass of **water**. What do you notice?

You could try this with **warm** water and **cold** water.

The **colour** of the water **changes** slowly as the blob of **paint** and the **water mix**.

What happens when we mix things with water?

Some things mix with water, others do not. Paint mixes with water, but pebbles do not.

Some things mix more easily with warm water than with cold water. Try mixing some salt or sugar with hot water. Then mix the same amount of salt or sugar with cold water. Do you notice a difference?

You could put a spoonful of cornflour or custard powder into a saucer. Slowly add drops of water and mix with your fingers. What do you notice? How does it feel?

If you stir **sand** in **water** it seems to mix. But if you wait, you will see the sand fall to the bottom, leaving clearer water above it.

If you **squash** a drink can or a plastic bottle, the **material** it is made from does not change but the **shape** changes.

The **amount** of plastic in the **squashed** bottle is the same as the amount of plastic in the **upright** bottle.

If you **crumple** a flat piece of paper into a ball, does the **amount** of paper change?

Which materials change shape?

It is possible to change the shape of some things by squashing, bending, twisting or stretching.

Some materials are used because their shape changes easily. If you bend a rubber or stretch an elastic band the shape changes, but can change back again.

Other materials are chosen to make things because their shape does not change easily. We use bricks to build houses and wood to make chairs and tables.

Foam changes **shape** when you squeeze it and springs back when you let it go. The **amount** of foam is the **same** after you have squeezed it as before.

Index